j567.9   Wenzel, Gregory C.
WEN
          Giant dinosaurs of
          the Jurassic.

$16.95   10/26/2004

DATE			

AR
BL: 6.0
pts: 0.5

Giant Dinosaurs
OF THE Jurassic

GREGORY WENZEL

Charlesbridge

To my friends Karen Snodgrass and
Brian Franczak—G. W.

Special thanks to Dr. James Kirkland, state
paleontologist with the Utah Geologic Survey

Published by Charlesbridge
85 Main Street
Watertown, MA 02472
(617) 926-0329
www.charlesbridge.com

Library of Congress Cataloging-in-Publication Data
Wenzel, Gregory C.
    Giant dinosaurs of the Jurassic / Gregory Wenzel.
        p. cm.
    Summary: Provides a look at the dinosaurs that lived in the
Morrison Formation in prehistoric Colorado and the world
in which they lived.
    ISBN 1-57091-563-6 (reinforced for library use)
    ISBN 1-57091-564-4 (softcover)
1. Dinosaurs—Juvenile literature. 2. Paleontology—Jurassic—
Juvenile literature. [1. Dinosaurs. 2. Paleontology—Jurassic.] I. Title.
QE861.5.W46 2004
567.9—dc22   2003015845

Printed in Korea
(hc) 10 9 8 7 6 5 4 3 2 1
(sc) 10 9 8 7 6 5 4 3 2 1

Illustrations done in acrylics on paper
Text and display type set in Adobe Goudy
Color separated, printed, and bound by Sung In Printing, Korea
Production supervision by Linda Jackson
Designed by Susan Mallory Sherman

Visitors Center,
Dinosaur National
Monument

Morrison, CO

Boundaries of the Morrison Formation ▬▬▬

In 1877 paleontologists found the remains of one of the largest animals that has ever lived: an 80-foot-long (24.4 meters) giant dinosaur that bone hunter Othniel Marsh named *Apatosaurus*. *Apatosaurus* was one of the long-necked giant dinosaurs called sauropods that lived during the late Jurassic period, 150 million years ago.

Layers of rock from this time period in North America are called the Morrison Formation, after the town of Morrison, Colorado. Since Marsh's time, bones of Jurassic dinosaurs have been dug from hundreds of quarries across the American West. It is the richest collection of dinosaur specimens from any era.

Skeletal material from hundreds of dinosaurs has been collected from Morrison locations. One quarry, Dinosaur National Monument, has produced more complete dinosaur skeletons than any other location in North America.

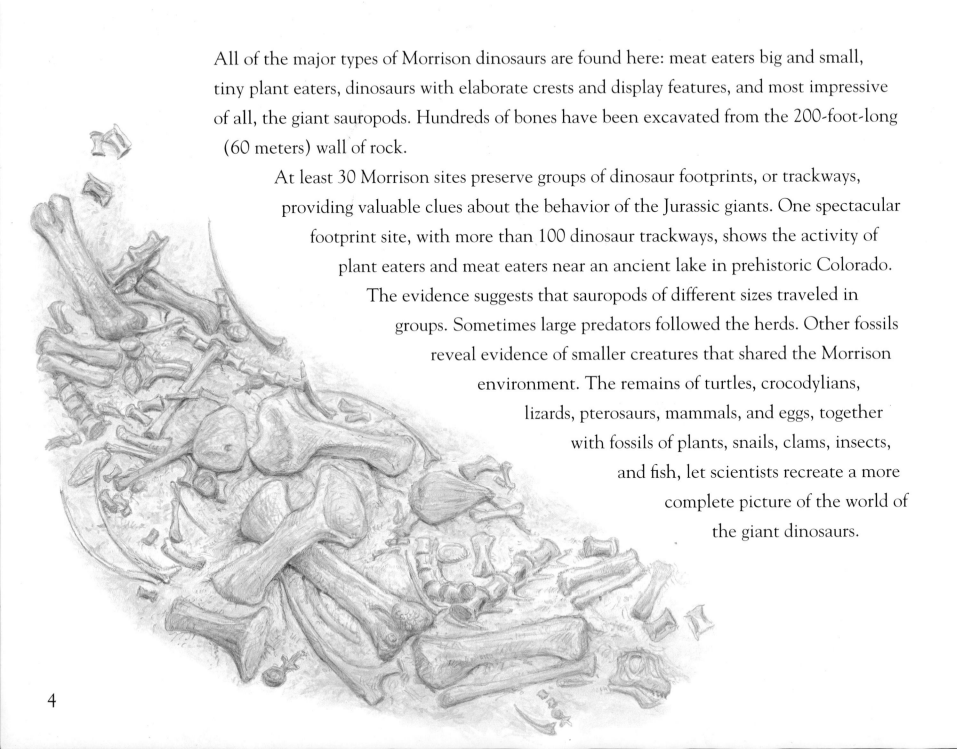

All of the major types of Morrison dinosaurs are found here: meat eaters big and small, tiny plant eaters, dinosaurs with elaborate crests and display features, and most impressive of all, the giant sauropods. Hundreds of bones have been excavated from the 200-foot-long (60 meters) wall of rock.

At least 30 Morrison sites preserve groups of dinosaur footprints, or trackways, providing valuable clues about the behavior of the Jurassic giants. One spectacular footprint site, with more than 100 dinosaur trackways, shows the activity of plant eaters and meat eaters near an ancient lake in prehistoric Colorado. The evidence suggests that sauropods of different sizes traveled in groups. Sometimes large predators followed the herds. Other fossils reveal evidence of smaller creatures that shared the Morrison environment. The remains of turtles, crocodylians, lizards, pterosaurs, mammals, and eggs, together with fossils of plants, snails, clams, insects, and fish, let scientists recreate a more complete picture of the world of the giant dinosaurs.

If we could stand in Colorado and run time backward 150 million years, we would see the Rocky Mountains flatten and then disappear. In their place, open forests of araucaria trees grow. Beyond them stretch vast fern prairies dotted with cycads. A huge river cuts through the Morrison landscape. But it is the dry season now, and the river no longer flows. Only isolated pools are left. One of these pools has become an oasis for the animals living near it.

The need for water brings animals together. Under the baking sun, aquatic creatures cluster in the dwindling water hole. In the shallows, the bulbous eyes of frogs poke through the surface. Huge river turtles, five feet long (1.5 meters), pull themselves through the mud at the edge of the pool. Long-tailed pterosaurs called *Comodactylus* swoop down, using needlelike teeth to snatch trapped fish. Ten-foot-long (3 meters) *Goniopholis* sprawl at the water's edge. These crocodylians feed on fish, as well as on small dinosaurs that come to drink.

On the wide, muddy shore, two *Othnielia* stop to drink from a gigantic, water-filled sauropod footprint. The three-foot-long (0.9 meter) plant-eating dinosaurs stay beyond the water hole's edge to avoid being attacked by the *Goniopholis*. They drink their fill, then groom themselves with their horny beaks.

. . . Comodactylus swoop down, using needlelike teeth . . .

An *Ornitholestes* appears and the two *Othnielia* dash away, chirping an alarm at the intruder. It is too hot for the *Ornitholestes* to pursue them. The hungry predator instead searches the dried-out carcass of a juvenile *Camarasaurus* for lizards and mammals that might be hiding there.

Six-foot-long (1.8 meters) *Ornitholestes* is one of the theropods, a group of animals that includes meat-eating dinosaurs and birds. *Ornitholestes* looks like a bird, with hairlike feathers, a long, thin neck, and long legs. With a powerful bite and clawed, grasping hands, *Ornitholestes* specializes in hunting small game.

Approaching the carcass, the *Ornitholestes* sees movement. A small mammal, a *Docodont*, tries to catch an insect. The theropod stalks its prey. But the unexpected sight of a *Stegosaurus*, come to visit the water hole, distracts the hunter before it can strike. The *Docodont* sees its danger, scampers under a bone, and escapes.

. . . chirping an alarm at the intruder . . .

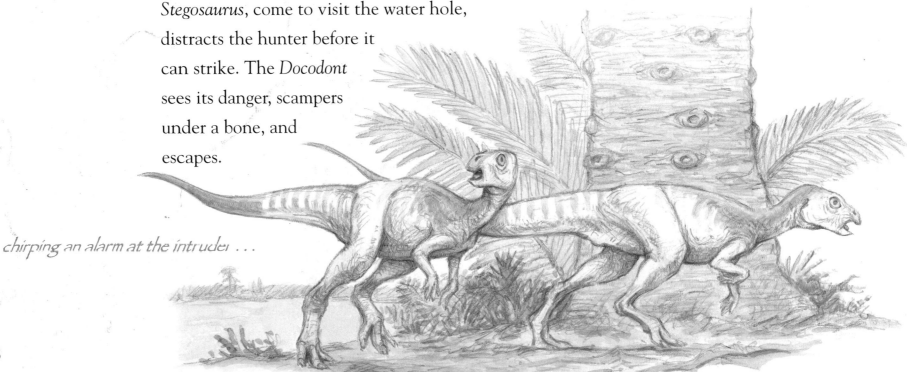

8

The *Stegosaurus* wades into the water hole to drink. At 25 feet long (7.5 meters), the elaborately plated dinosaur is too big to be attacked by crocodylians.

Stegosaurus is the most spectacular of the Morrison dinosaurs. Seventeen plates in two staggered rows run along its back, the tallest more than three feet high (0.9 meter). Near the end of its tail, two long spikes stick straight out on either side. The plates and spikes are covered with smooth, shiny, hard keratin, like a turtle's shell. The plates are for display, making *Stegosaurus* appear larger, but the tail spikes can be used for defense.

A group of *Camptosaurus* joins the *Stegosaurus* at the water. Watching for crocodylians, they lower their beaked heads to drink. The 16-foot-long (4.8 meters) adult *Camptosaurus* are safe from attack, but juveniles could be killed by the big reptiles. When a *Goniopholis* floats nearby, the whole group scatters.

. . . the whole group scatters . . .

A group of sauropods, called *Camarasaurus*, dines on tall bushes and trees in the nearby araucaria wood. Standing on four stout legs, *Camarasaurus* can stretch its flexible neck to eat plants growing at different levels. Though the smallest of the Morrison sauropods, it can grow to 70 feet long (21.3 meters) and weigh 30 tons (27,000 kilograms).

Because of its size, *Camarasaurus* spends most of its time eating. Like other sauropods, it doesn't chew its food: blunt snouts rimmed with spoon-shaped teeth strip off mouthfuls of vegetation. The leafy matter is swallowed whole, then broken up and digested in the stomach.

Sauropods are messy eaters. As they forage, bits of foliage—even whole branches—drop to the ground. The *Othnielia* and *Camptosaurus* move carefully under the *Camarasaurus* to feed on the dropped leaves.

. . . bits of foliage drop to the ground . . .

Nearby, a *Brachiosaurus* browses in the forest canopy. This enormous sauropod is designed to feed in the tallest trees, well above the reach of its smaller relative *Camarasaurus*. Unlike most dinosaurs, *Brachiosaurus*'s front limbs are longer than its hind limbs, raising its back like a giraffe's. Powerful muscles raise and lower its 35-foot-long (11 meters) neck, so it can reach foliage 45 feet (14 meters) above the ground.

It takes an incredible amount of food to sustain these 60-ton, 90-foot-long (54,000 kilograms, 28 meters) giants, so *Brachiosaurus* aren't as common as other Morrison sauropods. Constantly eating, *Brachiosaurus* barely looks down as a meat eater, *Ceratosaurus*, passes by its gigantic legs. Due to its size, a full-grown *Brachiosaurus* is immune from attack, even by the largest predators. Unconcerned, the sauropod continues its meal.

. . . a meat eater passes by its gigantic legs . . .

In the heat of midday, the 30-foot-long (9 meters) *Ceratosaurus* searches the muddy rim of the water hole for prey. On the end of its snout is a bladelike horn, which might be used to attract the opposite sex or to intimidate rivals. As it hunts, groups of *Camptosaurus* around the water hole watch intently, jostling one another as they try to keep their distance.

Suddenly the theropod lunges at the closest *Camptosaurus*, and the herd scatters. Some splash into the water; others flee into the underbrush. The plant eaters are faster and more nimble, but *Ceratosaurus* is an excellent hunter. The chase is short: one *Camptosaurus* slips in the mud and falls. Powerful jaws clamp onto its tail. Violently shaking its victim, the *Ceratosaurus* kills the animal swiftly. The attack is over.

As the hunter begins to feed, life around the water hole returns to normal.

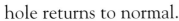

. . . violently shaking its victim . . .

Out on the floodplain, two *Dryosaurus*, 12-foot-long (3.6 meters) plant-eating dinosaurs, tend their nest. The nest, a shallow bowl scraped from the soil, contains 18 eggs. A mound of sand and vegetation shades the eggs from the sun. *Dryosaurus* are good parents, constantly working to keep their eggs from overheating.

Many of the eggs have already hatched. The babies can walk soon afterward, but they often stay close to the nest, where their parents bring them chewed-up plants to eat. The adult *Dryosaurus* work hard to protect their young from dangers.

A *Fruitachampsa*, a three-foot-long (0.9 meters) crocodylian with long legs, enters the nesting ground looking for eggs and hatchlings. The adult *Dryosaurus* squawk and threaten the *Fruitachampsa*, but the crocodylian is careful to avoid the *Dryosaurus*' painful bite. With a quick lunge, the intruder snatches a hatchling that wandered away from its parents. When the *Fruitachampsa* has left with its meal, the *Dryosaurus* return to their routine.

. . . the intruder snatches a hatchling . . .

A herd of *Apatosaurus* migrates across the fern prairie toward the water. Their feet stir up dust and insects, attracting flocks of flying reptiles called *Mesadactylus*. Some ride on the sauropods' backs, plucking off biting insects.

The dust-covered plants are poor fodder for these 80-foot-long, 30-ton sauropods (24.4 meters, 27,000 kilograms). The *Apatosaurus* have squared-off muzzles, just right for cropping vegetation, but they will wait to feed on the greener plants that grow near the water hole. Compared with their relatives *Camarasaurus* or

Brachiosaurus, Apatosaurus have longer and thinner tails and usually hold their necks lower to the ground. While on the move, they often lift their tiny heads to watch for predators.

The group of *Apatosaurus* attracts the attention of a curious *Allosaurus*. Flexing their necks, the sauropods keep an eye on the hunter as it passes near the herd. The *Allosaurus* stays clear of the adults' lashing, multi-ton tails and jogs off to find smaller prey at the riverbed. The *Apatosaurus* continue on.

The *Allosaurus's* sudden appearance at the water hole agitates the dinosaurs gathered there. Striding swiftly across the cracked mud on powerful legs, the theropod scans the area for prey.

Allosaurus is the largest Morrison predator, reaching lengths of 40 feet (12 meters). Its robust arms and enormous, curved claws are designed to grasp and hold prey. With a mouthful of sharp teeth and a muscular neck, *Allosaurus* can rip great chunks of meat from its victims.

The *Allosaurus* ignores the *Stegosaurus* and its dangerous spiked tail. Nearby is a heavily armored, seven-foot-long (2 meters) *Mymoorapelta*. The plant eater's body is protected with keratin-covered bones called scutes, and its sides and tail are lined with flat, triangular plates. Even the head and legs of *Mymoorapelta* are covered with horns and overlapping scales. The *Allosaurus* searches for a less thorny meal.

. . . its dangerous spiked tail . . .

At the water hole, dragonflies and other insects fill the air. The *Stegosaurus*, *Mymoorapelta*, *Othnielia*, and *Camptosaurus* cluster around the muddy edge, joined by several thirsty *Barosaurus*.

Standing on dry ground, the *Barosaurus* arch their long necks out over the water. Their tiny heads dip into the pool and suck up gallons of liquid. Nostrils placed high on their heads keep clear of the water while they drink. *Barosaurus* is as massive as its relative *Apatosaurus*, but its neck is nearly twice as long.

Although their size protects them from the *Allosaurus*, the *Barosaurus* are uneasy while it hunts. The meat eater approaches, eyeing a young sauropod. As the hunter circles, a large adult *Barosaurus* rears up, heaving its forelimbs off the ground and raising its 30-foot-long (9 meters) neck high in the air. Its attempt blocked, the *Allosaurus* looks for smaller prey.

. . . arch their long necks out over the water . . .

The *Othnielia* and the *Camptosaurus* remain motionless and alert in the presence of the *Allosaurus*. Small, lightly built *Othnielia* is too fast for the big predator to catch. Larger, bulkier *Camptosaurus* would make a good meal. But the *Allosaurus* does not attack.

Instead, it sees the *Ceratosaurus* feeding on the *Camptosaurus* it had killed earlier. The *Allosaurus* knows that stealing a meal is far easier than chasing one.

The *Allosaurus* moves to claim the carcass from the smaller theropod. The predators face off, growling and baring jaws of sharp, curved teeth. The one-sided contest is over quickly. After a brief, mostly vocal squabble, the outmatched *Ceratosaurus* snatches a hind leg from the *Camptosaurus* and runs off. The *Allosaurus*, satisfied with its prize, squats down and eats its fill.

. . . remain motionless and alert . . .

26

Thick, wet clouds blow across a darkening sky, and a crash of thunder echoes across the land. Cycad leaves clatter in a sudden cool breeze. Fat drops of rain begin to fall. The dry, cracked mud of the riverbed sucks up the water. The rain strikes the face of the *Allosaurus*, who looks up, momentarily distracted from its meal.

A lone 110-foot-long (33.5 meters) *Diplodocus*, ambling down the dry riverbed toward the water hole, stops as the rain falls more heavily. Even longer than its relatives *Apatosaurus* and *Barosaurus*, *Diplodocus* weighs up to 40 tons (36,000 kilograms). The sauropod bellows contentedly as the downpour soaks its dry, scaly skin. The rainy season has finally begun.

During the dry season, bodies of dead animals would lie about the Morrison plains, usually close to the water holes. Most skeletons fell apart or were scattered by scavengers, but a few were still complete when the rains began. Only those quickly buried would become fossils.

Torrential rains and floods washed the carcasses into wide, flowing rivers. The swift current tumbled the remains, pulling many of them apart. Small bones were carried away, while larger ones were deposited on sandbars or bends in the river. The bones and skeletons piled up and were buried in layers of fine sediment.

After millions of years, the sediment turned into layers of stone buried deep in the earth's crust. Slowly the rocks above the entombed Morrison animals eroded, and the ancient bones began to reemerge.

Paleontologists work hard to free these remains embedded in rock. They must proceed carefully, because the bones are very fragile and their size makes them hard to handle. Many sauropod bones are larger and heavier than the people who dig them up. Eventually the bones are sent to museums, where they are cleaned, studied, and sometimes displayed.

After more than a century of excavating Morrison quarries, paleontologists are still making new discoveries. The fossil skeleton of *Mymoorapelta* was found just a few years ago. Tantalizing fragments of Morrison dinosaurs hint at the existence of tiny feathered meat eaters, new varieties of armored plant eaters, and giant dinosaurs larger than any previously known. As long as there are new discoveries, scientists will keep looking and digging. Who knows what extraordinary Jurassic giants they will find in the future?

Glossary / Index

Author's Note

Dinosaur discoveries are happening all the time. Even as I worked on this book, a new specimen of *Stegosaurus* was being excavated in Montana by the Judith River Dinosaur Institute, an organization I've been lucky enough to work with as a staff member.

Portraying the daily lives of Jurassic dinosaurs takes more than just imagination. First I look at fossils that show evidence of behavior, such as trackways or nesting sites. Next I study what is known about the ancient Morrison environment. Finally I combine these clues with direct observation of the behavior of modern animals, particularly birds (which are living dinosaurs), allowing me to make educated assumptions about the activities of those long-extinct creatures.

A note on pronunciation: Scientific names of plants and animals are made by combining two or more Latin, Greek, or other root words. Pronouncing these names isn't easy, and many dinosaur experts don't always agree on the "right" way to do it. The pronunciations listed here keep the root words separate and distinct, to help you find similarities among the names.